75 Garlic Bread Recipes

(75 Garlic Bread Recipes - Volume 1)

Alice Francis

Copyright: Published in the United States by Alice Francis/ © ALICE FRANCIS

Published on October, 12 2020

All rights reserved. No part of this publication may be reproduced, stored in retrieval system, copied in any form or by any means, electronic, mechanical, photocopying, recording or otherwise transmitted without written permission from the publisher. Please do not participate in or encourage piracy of this material in any way. You must not circulate this book in any format. ALICE FRANCIS does not control or direct users' actions and is not responsible for the information or content shared, harm and/or actions of the book readers.

In accordance with the U.S. Copyright Act of 1976, the scanning, uploading and electronic sharing of any part of this book without the permission of the publisher constitute unlawful piracy and theft of the author's intellectual property. If you would like to use material from the book (other than just simply for reviewing the book), prior permission must be obtained by contacting the author at author@bisquerecipes.com

Thank you for your support of the author's rights.

Content

75 AWESOME GARLIC BREAD RECIPES 5

1. American Garlic Bread Recipe 5
2. Artisan Garlic Bread With Mozzarella Recipe 5
3. Authentic Italian Garlic Toast Recipe 5
4. Banana Bread Recipe 6
5. Basil Garlic Focaccia Bread Recipe 6
6. Bleu Cheese Garlic Bread Recipe 7
7. Blue Cheese Garlic Bread Recipe 7
8. Bread Machine Garlic Bread Recipe 7
9. Caramelized Onion Garlic And Sesame Bread Recipe 8
10. Cheesey Garlic Bubble Bread Recipe 8
11. Cheesy Artichoke Garlic Bread Recipe 9
12. Cheesy Garlic Bread Recipe 9
13. Cheesy Onion And Garlic Bread Recipe .. 10
14. Easy Cheesy Pull Apart Garlic Rolls Recipe 10
15. Easy Garlic Bread Bites Recipe 11
16. Fancy Garlic Bread Recipe 11
17. GOOEY MOZZARELLA GARLIC BREAD Recipe 11
18. Garlic Bread 12
19. Garlic Bread Deluxe Recipe 12
20. Garlic Bread Recipe 12
21. Garlic Bread Roulade Recipe 13
22. Garlic Bread With Garlic & Herb Cheese Recipe 13
23. Garlic Bread With Herbs De Provence No Cheese Recipe 13
24. Garlic Bread On The Go Recipe 14
25. Garlic Bread With Mayo Cheddar Recipe. 14
26. Garlic Cheese Bread Recipe 14
27. Garlic Cheese Quick Bread Recipe 15
28. Garlic Cheese And Tomato Bread Bites Recipe 15
29. Garlic Knots Recipe 15
30. Garlic Lover's Pull Apart Bread Recipe 16
31. Garlic Naan Breads Recipe 16
32. Garlic Parmesan Monkey Bread Recipe ... 17
33. Garlic Pita Bread Recipe 17
34. Garlic Potato Bread Recipe 18
35. Garlic Walnut Bread With Rosemary Recipe 18
36. Garlic N Herb Monkey Bread Recipe 19
37. Good For You Garlic Bread Recipe 19
38. Gorgonzola Garlic Bread Recipe 20
39. Gourmet Garlic Bread Recipe 20
40. Green Olive And Garlic Bread Recipe 21
41. Grilled Garlic Bread Recipe 21
42. Grilled Garlic Cheese Bread Recipe 21
43. Herb Garlic Bread Recipe 22
44. Home Baked Garlic Naan Bread Recipe ... 22
45. Jiffy Cheesey Garlic Bread Recipe 23
46. Killer Garlic Bread Recipe 23
47. Lynne's Retro Garlic Bread Recipe 23
48. Mary Megans Garlic Bread Recipe 24
49. Marys Garlic Bread Recipe 24
50. Moms Delicious Garlic Bread Recipe 24
51. Onion And Garlic Bread Recipe 25
52. PROVOLONE GARLIC BREAD Recipe 25
53. Parmesan And Asiago Cheese Garlic Bread Recipe 25
54. Parmesan Garlic Bread Recipe 26
55. Parmesan And Asiago Cheese Garlic Bread Recipe 26
56. Quick Easy Garlic Bread Sticks Recipe 27
57. Quick Casserole Garlic Bread Recipe 28
58. Quick Garlic Cheese Bread Recipe 28
59. Quick Italian Garlic Bread Slices Recipe ... 28
60. Quick, Easy, Delicious Garlic Bread Recipe 29
61. Reenies Garlic Bread Recipe 29
62. Roasted Garlic Bread Recipe 30
63. Roasted Garlic Potato Bread Recipe 30
64. Roman Garlic Bread Recipe 30
65. Simple Garlic Bread Recipe 31
66. Soft Garlic Breadsticks Recipe 31
67. Sourdough Garlic Bread Recipe 31
68. Stuffed Garlic Spinach Bread Recipe 32
69. Summy Wummys Famous Garlic Bread Recipe 32
70. Tear N Share Garlic Pizza Bread By Hand Or Machine Recipe 33
71. The Best Ever Two Minute Fake Garlic Bread Recipe 33
72. Ukrainian Garlic Bread Puffs Recipe 34
73. Garlic Bread By The Slice Recipe 34
74. Garlic Cheese Bread Recipe 35

75. Roasted Garlic And Rosemary Bread Recipe 35

INDEX 36

CONCLUSION.. 38

75 Awesome Garlic Bread Recipes

***

1. American Garlic Bread Recipe

Serving: 8 | Prep: | Cook: 10mins | Ready in:

Ingredients

- 10 medium cloves garlic with skins left on
- 6 tablespoons unsalted butter softened
- 2 tablespoons grated parmesan cheese
- 1/2 teaspoon salt
- 1 pound loaf Italian bread halved lengthwise
- 1/2 teaspoon freshly ground black pepper

Direction

- Adjust oven rack to middle position and heat oven to 500.
- Toast garlic cloves in small skillet over medium heat shaking pan occasionally for 8 minutes.
- When cool enough to handle skin and mince cloves.
- Using fork mash garlic, butter, cheese and salt in small bowl until thoroughly combined.
- Spread cut sides of loaf evenly with butter mixture then season with pepper.
- Transfer loaf halves buttered side up onto rimmed baking sheet.
- Bake reversing position of baking sheet in oven from front to back halfway through.
- Bake until golden brown and toasted about 10 minutes.
- Cut each half into 2" slices and serve immediately.

2. Artisan Garlic Bread With Mozzarella Recipe

Serving: 6 | Prep: | Cook: 5mins | Ready in:

Ingredients

- 1 can pizza crust (I use Pillsbury)
- 3-4 tbsp basil pesto (fresh or store-bought is fine!)
- 2 tbsp red crushed pepper (or to taste, but don't be a wuss!)
- 1 cup reduced-fat shredded mozzarella (I use Sargento)
- 3-4 tbsp parmigiana (I use Sargento)
- fresh basil leaves (optional)
- PAM olive oil flavor

Direction

- Preheat oven 425 degrees.
- Spray a round or rectangular baking sheet with PAM and open pizza crust. Spread onto baking sheet, making sure to unfold every corner.
- Spread pesto all over the crust, making sure to cover every inch. You want that robust pesto flavor in EVERY bite!
- Sprinkle red crushed pepper and top with cheeses, making sure to spread to every corner.
- Bake until crispy and golden brown and cheese is melted. Cut into small rectangles and serve with a side of pesto or marinara!

3. Authentic Italian Garlic Toast Recipe

Serving: 1 | Prep: | Cook: 5mins | Ready in:

Ingredients

- 1 sturdy stick of Italian bread (ideally made with semolina flour)
- Peeled raw garlic cloves (amount to be determined)
- Olive oil (use a good quality)

Direction

- Slice bread open, portion, and toast till very crispy.
- Rub raw garlic clove(s) on toasted bread to desired taste.
- Drizzle with olive oil.
- That's it, nothing but an uncomplicated taste of toasted bread, garlic, and fruity olive oil. Enjoy!

4. Banana Bread Recipe

Serving: 0 | Prep: | Cook: 15mins | Ready in:

Ingredients

- 1 1/2 cups bananas, mashed 375 ml
- 2 cups demerara sugar 500 ml
- 2 tsp lemon juice 10 ml
- 1 tsp sea salt 5 ml
- 2 eggs -
- 2/3 cup canola oil 160 ml
- 3/4 cup 2% milk 180 ml
- 2 1/2 cups unbleached white flour 625 ml
- 1 1/3 tsp baking soda 8 ml

Direction

- Preheat oven to 375°F degrees. Prepare two 9" x 5" loaf pans.
- In a mixer or bowl, combine bananas and sugar. Mix well.
- Add salt and lemon juice and mix.
- Add eggs, mixing on low speed.
- Add oil, milk, flour and soda; mix on low speed until combined.
- Pour into two greased loaf pans and bake at 375°F degrees for 1 hour or until done. For last 15 minutes cover with foil to prevent bread from getting too dark. Yields 2 loaves.

5. Basil Garlic Focaccia Bread Recipe

Serving: 6 | Prep: | Cook: 20mins | Ready in:

Ingredients

- 3/4 cup warm fat-free milk (70-80 degrees)
- 1/4 cup warm water (70-80 degrees)
- 1/4 cup soft butter
- 1 egg
- 2-3/4 cup flour
- 2 tbsp sugar
- 2 tsp kosher salt (divided)
- 2 tsp active dry yeast
- 4 tsp olive oil
- 1 tbsp garlic powder or 4 garlic cloves minced well
- 1 tbsp basil (or season of choice, rosemary, oregano, etc)
- 1 tbsp parmesan cheese

Direction

- In bread maker (follow bread maker instructions on order of adding ingredients).
- Place milk, water, butter (cut up), egg, flour, sugar, 1 tsp. salt and yeast (I also added 1 tsp. garlic powder).
- Select dough setting.
- Check after 5 minutes of mixing (I found the times I made this I added about 1 cup more of flour).
- When cycle is complete, turn dough onto lightly floured surface, and punch down.
- Cover and let it rest for 10 to 30 minutes.
- Shape into circle or rectangle (do not make too thin),
- Place on a baking pan (lightly covered with olive oil) and cover.
- Let is rise to doubled.

- Using a wood spoon handle, make intentions about 1/4" indents in dough.
- Brush with olive oil (4 tbsp.).
- Mix salt, garlic, basil together and sprinkle over top of bread.
- Sprinkle parmesan cheese over top (add more if you like).
- Bake 400 oven for 15-20 minutes or until golden brown, (if oven cooks quickly, watch, you do not want to burn or undercook).
- Cut into wedges or squares.

6. Bleu Cheese Garlic Bread Recipe

Serving: 2 | Prep: | Cook: 10mins | Ready in:

Ingredients

- 2 slices of Sara Lee sourdough bread
- 2 TBSP Bleu cheese dressing (or ranch dressing)
- margarine or butter(I use unsalted butter)
- garlic powder
- Shredded parmesan cheese
- parsley flakes

Direction

- Turn oven on BROIL.
- Spread margarine (or butter) evenly.
- Sprinkle garlic powder.
- Pour approx. 1 tbsp. bleu cheese dressing (or ranch) on each slice, spread evenly.
- Sprinkle parsley flakes on each slices.
- Sprinkle cheese evenly on each slices.
- Put in oven on bottom rack for approx. 5 mins till cheese melted, than move up to top rack close to the broil burner, broil for approx. 5 mins to till cheese bubbly and golden brown, Don't leave the kitchen too long as it will broil faster on top rack.
- Cut slices in half and serve with spaghetti.
- Enjoy!!

7. Blue Cheese Garlic Bread Recipe

Serving: 8 | Prep: | Cook: 15mins | Ready in:

Ingredients

- 1 loaf French bread or french baguette
- 1 stick unsalted butter at room temp.
- 8 oz. blue cheese, crumbled
- 2 TB minced garlic (or more to taste)

Direction

- Cut bread in half lengthwise.
- Mix butter, blue cheese and garlic together.
- Spread cheese mixture on each bread half.
- Place bread on a foil-lined cookie sheet.
- Bake at 350 degrees for 10 minutes.
- Broil for 3-5 minutes.
- Slice and enjoy!
- You can also wrap the bread in foil and grill for 15-20 minutes.

8. Bread Machine Garlic Bread Recipe

Serving: 6 | Prep: | Cook: 60mins | Ready in:

Ingredients

- 1 cup warm water (110 degrees F)
- 1 tablespoon butter
- 1 tablespoon dry milk powder
- 1 tablespoon white sugar
- 1 1/2 teaspoons salt
- 1 1/2 tablespoons dried parsley
- 2 teaspoons garlic powder
- 3 cups bread flour
- 2 teaspoons active dry yeast

Direction

- Place ingredients in the pan of the bread machine in the order recommended by the manufacturer. Select Basic Bread cycle; press Start.

9. Caramelized Onion Garlic And Sesame Bread Recipe

Serving: 16 | Prep: | Cook: 40mins | Ready in:

Ingredients

- 1 1/2 cups thinly sliced red onion
- 1 tbsp olive oil
- 1 tsp toasted sesame oil (optional but highly reccommended!)
- 1 package active dry yeast (about 1 1/4 tsp)
- 1 tbsp sugar
- 1 cup warm water
- 2 cups flour, divided
- 1 tsp gluten flour
- 1 cup whole wheat flour
- 3 tbsp garlic granules
- 1/2 tsp freshly ground pepper
- 1 tsp salt

Direction

- In a medium sauce pan, cook onions and oil over medium-high heat until onions are translucent.
- Reduce the heat to medium and cook until onions are light golden, about 15-20 minutes. Stir in the sesame oil and cook 1-2 minutes further.
- Remove from heat, cool to room temperature.
- In a large mixing bowl (or the bowl of a stand mixer), combine yeast, sugar and 1/4 cup water. Let stand until foamy, about 5-10 minutes.
- Add remaining water, mixing well.
- In another bowl, mix together 1 cup flour, gluten, whole wheat flour, garlic, pepper and salt.
- Add this mixture to the wet mix in the bowl and beat well to blend.
- Stir in onions.
- Add remaining flour gradually until dough comes together into an elastic ball (you may need more or less).
- Knead until smooth and elastic, about 5-7 minutes.
- Place dough in a greased bowl, and let rise 1 hour.
- Preheat oven to 350F. Lightly grease a 9x5" loaf pan.
- Gently deflate risen dough, shape into a loaf and place in the loaf pan.
- Cover with greased Cling Wrap and let rise about 45 minutes.
- Bake on the bottom shelf of the oven for 30 - 40 minutes, until dark gold.
- Cool on a wire rack before slicing.

10. Cheesey Garlic Bubble Bread Recipe

Serving: 6 | Prep: | Cook: 35mins | Ready in:

Ingredients

- 1 pound loaf frozen bread dough, thawed
- ½ cup garlic infused oil (you can make your own by simply putting several cloves of peeled garlic into a jar of good olive oil and allowing it to set for a few days)
- ½ cup butter
- 2 tablespoon finely minced fresh parsley
- 2 tablespoon finely minced fresh garlic (or run it through a garlic press)
- sea salt, to taste
- pepper, to taste
- ½ cup goat cheese, cubed or in pieces
- ½ cup fresh grated parmesan cheese
- additional garlic infused olive oil and grated parmesan cheese for serving

Direction

- Generously spray a 9x5 loaf pan with cooking spray (or I've used a deep, round casserole dish as well). You need a pan deep enough to create the layers, but not so deep that the bread can't bake all the way through in the allotted time.
- Pull off pieces of bread dough into small chunks - I just use a kitchen shears to cut it into small balls, about 1½" diameter – spray shears with cooking spray and it won't stick to the dough.
- In a small bowl, whisk together oil and butter, parsley and garlic.
- Dip dough balls in oil/butter mixture and arrange in layers in loaf pan.
- Sprinkle salt and pepper in between layers, and dot with goat cheese and some Parmesan.
- Finish top layer with a dusting of salt, pepper and grated Parmesan cheese, keeping all the goat cheese in the interior layers.
- When layers are complete, cover pan loosely with plastic wrap or waxed paper and allow bread to rise until doubled (takes close to an hour).
- Bake bread at 350 degrees for about 30 to 40 minutes, until browned and crusty on top.
- Cool bread about 15 minutes before serving. Don't try to slice it, but rather pull it apart in chunks to serve.
- Drizzle some of the garlic infused olive oil on a plate and sprinkle with some fresh grated Parmesan cheese; sprinkle with a little salt and pepper, if desired.
- Dip warm bread pieces into the oil/cheese mixture.

11. Cheesy Artichoke Garlic Bread Recipe

Serving: 6 | Prep: | Cook: 20mins | Ready in:

Ingredients

- 1 long loaf (12 oz.) seeded Italian bread, halved hoizontally
- 1 can (14 oz) artichoke hearts, drained, chopped
- 1/2 c mayonnaise
- 1 jar sliced pimentos, drained, chopped
- 1/4 c shredded parmesan cheese
- 1/4 c chopped, fresh chives
- 1 Tbs Dijon mustard
- 2 cloves garlic, minced
- 1/3 c shredded mozzarella cheese
- 3 Tbs Italian -seasoned bread crumbs
- 1 tsp olive oil

Direction

- Preheat oven to 400. Line jellyroll pan with foil. Place bread halves, cut sides up, on pan. In bowl, combine artichoke hearts, mayonnaise, pimentos, Parmesan, chives, mustard and garlic.
- Spread artichoke mixture over bread; sprinkle with mozzarella.
- In small bowl, combine breadcrumbs and oil; sprinkle over mozzarella. Bake 15 to 20 mins or till lightly browned and heated through. Cool slightly; cut each bread half crosswise into 6 pieces.

12. Cheesy Garlic Bread Recipe

Serving: 8 | Prep: | Cook: 3mins | Ready in:

Ingredients

- 1 long loaf Italian bread
- 1 tbsp. butter
- splash Worchestershire sauce
- 1 tsp. minced garlic
- sprinkle of parmesan cheese to cover

Direction

- Cut loaf lengthwise then widthwise into chunks. In a small container, add butter, Worcestershire sauce and 1 tsp. minced garlic from a jar. Mix well and spread on bread slices, place on cookie sheet and sprinkle with grated parmesan cheese. Broil until just crispy and serve.

13. Cheesy Onion And Garlic Bread Recipe

Serving: 8 | Prep: | Cook: 20mins | Ready in:

Ingredients

- 1 tablespoon butter
- ¾ cup finely diced onion
- 3 medium cloves fresh garlic, diced finely (I have to say that the jarred diced garlic doesn't give me the same wonderful flavor as the freshly diced or pressed garlic - just my opinion!)
- ½ cup half-and-half or whole milk
- 1 egg, beaten
- 1½ cups Bisquick mix
- 1 cup shredded sharp cheddar cheese, divided
- ½ teaspoon onion salt or garlic salt
- 2 tablespoons melted butter
- 1 tablespoon chopped fresh chives (this can be omitted, but it adds such nice color to the finished product!)

Direction

- Heat 1 tablespoon butter in a small skillet over medium heat.
- Add the onions and garlic; cook until tender and translucent.
- In a large bowl, add the milk and egg to the biscuit mix, stirring just until the mix is moistened.
- Gently fold in the onions and garlic, and ½ cup of the cheese.
- Spoon the dough into a greased 9 or 10 inch glass pie pan.
- Mix the onion or garlic salt into the 2 tablespoons melted butter and drizzle this over the dough.
- Sprinkle dough with chives.
- Bake at 400 degrees for 15 minutes.
- Top bread with remaining ½ cup cheese and continue baking until bread is done, about 5 minutes longer.
- Cut the bread into wedges and serve warm with butter (I've never found the extra butter necessary).

14. Easy Cheesy Pull Apart Garlic Rolls Recipe

Serving: 18 | Prep: | Cook: 20mins | Ready in:

Ingredients

- 2 (12 oz) tubes refrigerated biscuits
- 1 cup shredded mozzarella
- 1 cup shredded mild cheddar
- 8 Tbsp melted butter
- 3 Tbsp Parmesan cheese
- 1/2 Tbsp parsley
- 1 tsp garlic powder
- 1/4 tsp salt

Direction

- Preheat oven to 375°F.
- Cut biscuits into quarters, and place in a large bowl.
- Add the melted butter, and all other ingredients.
- Mix with your hands, coating all of the biscuit pieces.
- Place the pieces in a muffin tin, 4 pieces per tin (you'll have extra, just use them in whichever tins you want).
- Bake for 20 minutes. Best served fresh out of the oven.

15. Easy Garlic Bread Bites Recipe

Serving: 8 | Prep: | Cook: 12mins | Ready in:

Ingredients

- 1 can grands biscuits
- 1/2 stick butter
- 1 c shredded cheese, your choice
- 2 T chopped garlic
- italian seasoning

Direction

- Preheat oven according to biscuit package directions.
- Butter a 9" round cake pan.
- Cut each biscuit into 4ths with pizza cutter.
- Crowd into pan.
- Melt butter on stovetop.
- Stir in cheese, garlic and seasoning.
- Brush/pour over bread.
- Bake about 12 minutes, until golden brown.

16. Fancy Garlic Bread Recipe

Serving: 6 | Prep: | Cook: 12mins | Ready in:

Ingredients

- 6 to 8 large garlic cloves, chopped
- 1/4 cup chopped flat-leaf parsley
- 1/4 cup chopped fresh oregano leaves
- 1/2 teaspoon kosher salt (it seems like a lot of salt, so maybe go a little light, but the salty flavor is what makes it.)
- Freshly ground black pepper
- 1/2 cup olive oil
- 1 loaf of your favorite grocery store bread. Pick something crusty, like ciabatta. I always use this Portugese Salaio bread they have at my grocery store. Just think crusty italian-type bread
- 2 tablespoons unsalted butter...I use olivio or something margarine-like

Direction

- Preheat the oven to 350 degrees F.
- Place the peeled, whole garlic cloves in the bowl of a food processor and process until minced.
- Add the parsley, oregano, salt and pepper and pulse a few times till it starts to look kind of pesto like. Not totally blended though.
- Heat the olive oil in a medium sauté pan and add the garlic mixture. Remove the pan from the heat.
- Slice the bread in half horizontally, and spread the butter on top half. Spread the garlic mixture on the bottom half of the bread, and put the halves together.
- Wrap the bread in aluminum foil.
- Place the bread in the oven and bake for 5 minutes. Open the foil, and continue baking for an additional 5 minutes.
- Cut into slices and enjoy! Trust me, there will be no left overs!

17. GOOEY MOZZARELLA GARLIC BREAD Recipe

Serving: 610 | Prep: | Cook: 15mins | Ready in:

Ingredients

- 1 loaf Italian or French bread, halved crosswise
- 1 to 2 tablespoons olive oil
- 1 1/2 teaspoons garlic powder
- 1 cup shredded mozzarella (regular or part-skim)

Direction

- Preheat oven to 400 degrees F.
- Brush olive oil all over bottom half of bread. Sprinkle garlic over oil. Top with cheese and close bread, as if making a sandwich.
- Wrap bread in foil and bake 10 to 15 minutes, until cheese melts.

18. Garlic Bread

Serving: 0 | Prep: | Cook: |Ready in:

Ingredients

- 1/2 cup butter, melted
- 3 to 4 garlic cloves, minced
- 1 loaf (1 pound) French bread, halved lengthwise
- 2 tablespoons minced fresh parsley

Direction

- In a small bowl, combine butter and garlic. Brush over cut sides of bread; sprinkle with parsley. Place, cut side up, on a baking sheet.
- Bake at 350° for 8 minutes. Broil 4-6 in. from the heat for 2 minutes or until golden brown. Cut into 2-in. slices. Serve warm.
- Garlic Bread Tips
- How do you store garlic bread?
- Leftover garlic bread can be wrapped tightly in foil and stored in the refrigerator for up to 3 days. To reheat, bake the wrapped bread at 350° for 10-15 minutes.
- What if I don't have fresh garlic?
- No garlic cloves? No problem! Substitute ½ teaspoon granulated garlic for every fresh clove called for in this garlic bread recipe.
- What are some perfect pairings for garlic bread?
- Garlic bread is a delicious side that naturally pairs well with recipes involving marinara, like our best-ever lasagna recipe. If you're looking for a meal that's lighter, serve garlic bread alongside tomato soup or Italian chopped salad. You can use up your leftovers in any of these recipes that start with garlic bread!
- Nutrition Facts
- 1 piece: 258 calories, 13g fat (7g saturated fat), 31mg cholesterol, 462mg sodium, 30g carbohydrate (1g sugars, 2g fiber), 5g protein.

19. Garlic Bread Deluxe Recipe

Serving: 12 | Prep: | Cook: 5mins |Ready in:

Ingredients

- 1 loaf Italian bread
- 4 large cloves garlic minced
- 1 stick butter, softened
- 3 Tbsp mayonaise
- 1/2 c fresh grated parmesan
- 1 tsp dried tarragon

Direction

- Preheat broiler.
- Split the loaf of Italian bread lengthwise.
- Mix together garlic, mayonnaise and butter until blended.
- Spread on the cut sides of the bread.
- Sprinkle cheese on top of garlic mixture, then sprinkle with tarragon.
- Place under broiler until bubbly and slightly browned.
- Slice and serve.

20. Garlic Bread Recipe

Serving: 4 | Prep: | Cook: 20mins |Ready in:

Ingredients

- 1 loaf of French, Italian or sourdough bread
- 5 tbsps. of butter or margarine, softened
- 2 tbsps.finely chopped parsley
- 2 green onions finely chopped
- 2 cloves minced garlic
- 1/2 tsp. dried basil ,crumbled until fine..
- 1/2 tsp. salt

Direction

- Pre-heat oven to 450.
- Cut the bread diagonally into 1 inch slices, almost to the bottom of the loaf.
- Mix up all of the other ingredients in a bowl and then butter both sides of the slices of bread, and the top crust.
- Wrap the loaf loosely with foil, put on a baking sheet and bake for about 15 mins.

21. Garlic Bread Roulade Recipe

Serving: 0 | Prep: | Cook: 20mins | Ready in:

Ingredients

- 1 lb of bread dough
- 1/2 cup of butter, softened
- 1/4 cup mozzarella cheese
- 1 tbsp minced garlic
- 1/4 cup parmesan cheese

Direction

- PREHEAT oven to 400F.
- Roll out the bread into a 9x13 rectangle.
- Spread the butter, leaving a one inch border on all sides.
- Evenly distribute the garlic, parmesan, and mozzarella.
- Roll from one long edge towards the other.
- Bake until cooked. (Time may vary)

22. Garlic Bread With Garlic & Herb Cheese Recipe

Serving: 0 | Prep: | Cook: 10mins | Ready in:

Ingredients

- 1 pkg. (6.5 oz.) Alouette garlic & herbs Spreadable cheese
- 1 loaf French bread, sliced
- 1 tbsp. fresh chopped parsley
- 2 tbsp. freshly grated parmesan cheese

Direction

- Preheat oven on Broil setting.
- Spread Alouette Garlic & Herbs Spreadable Cheese on slices of French bread.
- Sprinkle with parsley and parmesan cheese.
- Place on baking sheet and broil until cheese melts.
- Cut into portions and serve.

23. Garlic Bread With Herbs De Provence No Cheese Recipe

Serving: 2 | Prep: | Cook: 30mins | Ready in:

Ingredients

- 2 mini-bread loaves [rustic italian white bread] [LaBrea Bakery is good]
- One large Bulb garlic [Around 10 extra large cloves, the more the better]
- Extra-Virgin Cold Pressed olive oil
- herbs de Provence [McCormick blend works well]
- dill [fresh or dried; Dried used here]
- salt [to taste]
- Large Mixing Bowl

Direction

- Pre-Heat oven to at least 400 deg. F.
- Take your bread, I use mini-loaves made by La Brea Bakery from Costco.
- Slice each mini-loaf in half, end to end thru the center.
- Chop your garlic into pieces, medium-chunky is good.
- Add chopped Garlic, Herbs de Provence, Dill, and a couple of pinches of salt into mixing bowl. Coat with copious amount of Olive Oil and mix with hands. Make sure there is plenty of your herb mixture in there, you really will

- be hard pressed to overdo it. Also don't be shy with the olive oil. It's not going to kill you.
- Take garlic, herbs, and Olive Oil mixture and spread evenly over the top of each loaf with your fingers. You should have 4 surfaces to coat.
- Once each slice is coated evenly with the garlic & herbs, take the remaining mixture in your bowl and pour lightly over each loaf, coating the top of each piece with a liberal amount of olive oil.
- Place onto cooking sheet covered with tinfoil
- Bake at 400deg F, for 20-30 minutes, until edges of bread are golden brown.
- Remember, *no* cheese is used in this, *don't* panic! It's going to taste wonderful, I promise. They key is the copious amount of garlic which will sweeten as you bake it, releasing all its deliciousness into your mouth in a torrent of pleasure.

24. Garlic Bread On The Go Recipe

Serving: 4 | Prep: | Cook: 5mins | Ready in:

Ingredients

- 2 cloves of garlic crushed
- 2 tbl of butter
- 1tbl olive oil
- 1 loaf bread sliced diagonally
- 1tbl parsley finely chopped

Direction

- Crush the garlic and mix with the butter in a bowl.
- Add the parsley.
- Spread the butter on each slice of bread on one side.
- Heat the olive oil in a skillet/griddle pan.
- Add the slices of bread to the pan unbuttered side down.
- Lightly fry the bread on the one side until the bottom is crispy and the butter starts to melt.

- Serve warm.

25. Garlic Bread With Mayo Cheddar Recipe

Serving: 6 | Prep: | Cook: 6mins | Ready in:

Ingredients

- 1 loaf French bread, split or sliced
- 1 cup mayonnaise
- 2-3 cloves minced garlic
- 1/2 cup sweet onions, diced
- 1 cup grated cheddar cheese
- 3 tablespoons parmesan cheese
- 2 tablespoons fresh parsley, chopped fine
- 4 tablespoons half-and-half cream

Direction

- Mix mayonnaise and the next six ingredients in a small bowl.
- Spread on the split or sliced French bread and bake in the broiler approximately 5-6 minutes or until golden brown and bubbly.

26. Garlic Cheese Bread Recipe

Serving: 10 | Prep: | Cook: 14mins | Ready in:

Ingredients

- 1 pkg cream cheese
- 1 tbsp garlic salt
- 1 1/3 cup parmesan cheese
- 1 stick butter
- 1 tbsp parsley
- 1 loaf French bread

Direction

- Preheat the oven to 400.

- Mix all ingredients (except French bread) thoroughly.
- Slice French bread to desired thickness.
- Spread a nice amount on one side of the bread and place on a baking sheet.
- When done place in the oven and bake 12-14 minutes!

27. Garlic Cheese Quick Bread Recipe

Serving: 12 | Prep: | Cook: 65mins | Ready in:

Ingredients

- 3 cups self rising flour*
- 1 cup shredded sharp cheddar cheese
- 1/4 cup sugar
- 1 tsp garlic powder
- 1-1/2 cups milk
- 1/4 cup vegetable oil (I use canola oil)
- 1 egg

Direction

- Preheat oven to 350F. In a large bowl, combine flour, cheese, sugar and garlic powder. In another bowl, whisk the milk, oil and egg. Stir into dry ingredients until just moistened. Pour into a greased 9 x 5 loaf pan. Bake for 55 to 65 minutes or until a toothpick inserted near the center comes out clean. Cool for 10 minutes before removing from pan.
- *I never keep self-rising flour around. Substitute for each cup of self-rising flour:
- Place 1-1/2 tsp. baking powder and 1/2 tsp. salt into a measuring cup. Add all-purpose flour to measure 1 cup.

28. Garlic Cheese And Tomato Bread Bites Recipe

Serving: 10 | Prep: | Cook: 17mins | Ready in:

Ingredients

- 10 Pillsbury® frozen soft white dinner rolls (from 12.4-oz bag)
- 1 container (6.5 oz) garlic-and-herbs spreadable cheese
- 1 tablespoon diced sundried tomatoes
- 1 tablespoon diced pitted kalamata olives
- 1 jar (8 oz) marinara sauce, warmed

Direction

- 1. Heat oven to 375°F. Remove rolls from bag; thaw 10 minutes. With thumb, make indentation in center of each roll.
- 2. In medium bowl, mix cheese, sundried tomatoes and olives. Place 1 tablespoon cheese mixture in each indentation. Place on ungreased cookie sheet.
- 3. Bake 12 to 17 minutes or until tops are light golden brown. Serve with marinara sauce.
- High Altitude (3500-6500 ft.): No change.

29. Garlic Knots Recipe

Serving: 48 | Prep: | Cook: 2hours | Ready in:

Ingredients

- 1 pkg. yeast
- 1 cup water
- 1 T. sugar
- 4 cups flour
- 1 tsp salt
- 3 T. olive oil
- 4 to 5 lg. cloves garlic
- 1/2 cup olive oil
- 1/2 cup corn oil
- salt to taste
- garlic powder to taste

- 1/4 cup grated romano cheese

Direction

- Combine yeast, water and sugar in a bowl and allow to proof. Add the flour and salt and mix with an electric mixer until well combined. Add the olive oil. Knead for 10 minutes or until dough is smooth. Divide dough in half. Brush dough with a little extra olive oil on all sides and allow to rise in a shallow pan for 60 minutes, covered with plastic wrap and a cloth, or until double in size. Remove dough and place on a flat surface. Roll each piece out with a rolling pin into a 6x12 inch rectangle. Cut each into 2(3x12inch) rectangles. Cut each rectangle into 12x3x1 inch strips. Loosely form each strip into a knot taking care not to stretch the dough. Place formed knots 1 inch apart on a greased baking sheet and bake in a 400 degree oven for 10 to 15 minutes or until lightly browned on top. Remove, place in a large bowl. In a blender, process garlic with olive and corn oils until creamy. As soon as the garlic knots come out of the oven, drizzle them with 4 tablespoons of the oil mixture and toss two to three times. Sprinkle with salt and garlic powder and toss until knots are well coated. Sprinkle with Romano Cheese and toss once more.

30. Garlic Lover's Pull Apart Bread Recipe

Serving: 0 | Prep: | Cook: 1hours40mins | Ready in:

Ingredients

- * 7-8 cups of bread flour
- * 3 tbsp sugar
- * 2 tbsp garlic salt
- * 2 packages dry yeast (or 4 1/2 tsp)
- * 1 1/2 cup water
- * 1/2 cup milk
- * 1/4 cup butter
- * 2 tbsp italian seasonings
- * 6-10 cloves crushes garlic
- * 2 tbsp garlic powder
- For the topping:
- * 1/2 cup butter
- * 1 tbsp italian seasonings
- * 1 tbsp garlic
- * 1/4 tsp salt

Direction

- 1. Combine 6 cups flour, sugar, garlic salt and dry yeast together. Mix to let loose any lumps.
- 2. Meanwhile, in a medium sauce pan combine water, milk, butter, seasonings, garlic and garlic powder to a boil, but stirring during. Once hot, pour into flour mix. When you touch it shouldn't stick to your finger. Place in a warm area for an hour to let rise. Split your ball in half, because this recipe makes two loaves. Form an oval and make 2 slices the longer way and 3 the shorter way. Place in a well-greased loaf pan and bake for 30 min on 400.
- 3. Once out of the oven, melt your butter and mix in the rest of the ingredients for the topping. With a grilling brush, pastry brush or a spoon (brushes work better though) spread your butter mix on both loaves. I've even added in some Parmesan if you want a little cheesy flavor!

31. Garlic Naan Breads Recipe

Serving: 4 | Prep: | Cook: 5mins | Ready in:

Ingredients

- Here we go
- 3 cups all purpose flour
- 1tsp (somewhat heaped) yeast
- 1 head of grated raw garlic
- 1 tbsp sugar
- 1 tbsp salt
- 1 tbsp oil

- about 3/4 cups of milk (warm)
- about half a cup of (warm)
- seseme seeds handfull

Direction

- You want to make your yeast all bubbly by mixing it in warm water and sugar.
- Add the oil and salt to the flour and rub the oil in.
- Then started mixing the dough with the milk/water mixture. If you need more liquid add more water but I think this much should be ok.
- Add the grated garlic into the mixture.
- It's ok if your dough is very sticky, should not be dry.
- Leave it covered for 15/20 minutes (or as long as you can, few hours) in a warm place till it rises. (Double in volume)
- Then just take some dough and shape it into a ball. I did not roll the naan out with a rolling pin but just did it all with hands.
- Lay your naan on a buttered baking tray and pop them in the oven on grill/broil. Put the tray on the highest shelf. You barely need to bake them for two mins, keep an eye on them.
- Add tiny bits of butter and sesame seeds on top if desired so it melts while cooking
- Once they get golden brown on top which again doesn't take more than two mins u flip them over for a bit just to get the bottom part a little gold too and voila you're done!

32. Garlic Parmesan Monkey Bread Recipe

Serving: 10 | Prep: | Cook: 30mins | Ready in:

Ingredients

- 3 Tbs finely chopped green onions
- 3 Tbs parsley
- 1-1/2 tsp garlic powder
- 1/4 tsp salt
- 5 Tbs butter, melted
- 2 eggs
- 2 (1lb) loaves frozen bread dough, thawed
- 1/2 c parmesan cheese

Direction

- Grease 10" Bundt or tube pan.
- In medium bowl, mix together the green onion, parsley, garlic powder, salt, butter and eggs until well blended. Break bread dough off in walnut-sized pieces and dip each in egg mixture.
- Place coated dough balls into prepared pan. Once there is a layer of balls covering the bottom of the pan, sprinkle with parmesan cheese. Repeat, sprinkling each layer with cheese till everything is in the pan.
- Cover loosely, and let rise until doubled in size, about 45 mins. Preheat oven to 350 degrees.
- Bake 30 mins or till golden brown.

33. Garlic Pita Bread Recipe

Serving: 4 | Prep: | Cook: 15mins | Ready in:

Ingredients

- 2 teaspoons active dry yeast
- 1 tablespoon sugar
- 1 1/4 cups warm water (about 110 to 115°)
- 3 1/2 cups all-purpose flour
- 1/2 teaspoon salt
- 1 cup margarine or butter, melted
- 1 tablespoon garlic, minced
- 1/2 tablespoon dried parsley flakes
- oil

Direction

- Put yeast in 1/4 cup of the water; add sugar and let stand for 10 minutes.
- Sift 2 1/2 cups of flour and the salt into a warm bowl.

- Form a well in the center; pour in yeast mixture and remaining warm water.
- Begin to mix with hand, wooden spoon, or dough hook, adding remaining flour as needed.
- Turn out onto a floured surface and knead for about 10 to 15 minutes, until smooth and no longer sticky.
- Oil a large boil; place dough in bowl and turn to coat with oil.
- Cover with a damp cloth and put in a warm place free of drafts for 1 1/2 to 2 hours.
- Dough should be doubled in bulk. Knead for a few minutes then divide into balls about 2 1/2 inches in diameter.
- Roll balls into circles on a lightly floured surface with floured rolling pin, or flatten into circles with hand.
- The circles should be about 1/4-inch thick and about 7 inches in diameter.
- Sandwich the circles between floured cloths and let rise for about 20 minutes in a warm place.
- Preheat oven to 475°.
- Sprinkle cookie sheets with flour or oil.
- Place loaves on baking sheets and bake 5 to 10 minutes.
- If baking sheets are oiled, turn pita loaves to brown both sides.
- While pita baking, prepare melted margarine, garlic, and parsley, combine in a bowl.
- When Pita is done, and removed from oven, immediately brush on margarine mixture onto pita bread.
- Can serve warm or set on wire racks to cool.

34. Garlic Potato Bread Recipe

Serving: 1 | Prep: | Cook: 30mins | Ready in:

Ingredients

- 1 large potato, boiled and grated (1 1/2 cups)
- 1 tsp salt
- 1 large garlic clove, crushed
- 1 cup warm water from the cooking potato
- 1 pkg. dry yeast
- 2 tsp. sugar
- 2 cups flour
- softened butter

Direction

- In a bowl, combine the potato, salt, garlic, potato water, yeast, and sugar.
- Mix well.
- Stir in the flour and mix again.
- Turn the dough onto a board and knead smooth.
- Place in a buttered bowl and turn to coat the surface.
- Cover with plastic wrap and a towel. Let rise until doubled in bulk - about 1 hour.
- Punch down dough and shape in a ball.
- Place on baking sheet sprinkled with four or cornmeal where the bread will sit.
- Or bake the bread in an 8 or 9 inch skillet with an oven proof handle.
- Brush the bread with butter and let rise until double in bulk.
- Preheat oven to 450.
- Bake for 25-30 minutes or until golden brown.

35. Garlic Walnut Bread With Rosemary Recipe

Serving: 10 | Prep: | Cook: 55mins | Ready in:

Ingredients

- 1 cup warm milk
- 1 tbs active dry yeast
- 2 tsp sugar
- 1/2 cup rye flour
- 2 1/2 cups unbleached flour, plus more if needed
- 2 tsp kosher salt
- 1/4 tsp freshly ground white pepper

- 1 tbs minced fresh rosemary (2 tsp dried)
- 3 plump garlic cloves, smashed and minced
- 1/4 cup walnut oil
- 1/2 cup walnuts, coarsely chopped

Direction

- Combine 1/2 cup of milk, yeast, sugar in a small bowl. Blend well and let stand until foamy, about 5-10 minutes.
- Combine rye flour, 2 cups of unbleached flour, salt, pepper, rosemary and garlic in the bowl of an electric mixer (if mixing by hand, use a wooden spoon). In a medium-sized bowl, blend together remaining 1/2 cup milk, walnut oil, and yeast mixture.
- With mixer running on low, add milk mixture to flour mixture. Then add nuts. Blend well, adding more flour if dough is very wet and sticky.
- Knead dough for 7 to 10 minutes with a dough hook or 12 to 15 minutes by hand on a lightly floured board until smooth and elastic. Form dough into a smooth round.
- Lightly oil a large mixing bowl. (We prefer a large wooden salad bowl.) Turn dough over in bowl, coating it with oil. Cover bowl with plastic wrap and let rise in a warm place until doubled in volume, 2 to 3 hours.
- Lightly knead dough to eliminate any bubbles. Shape into a round and place on an oiled pizza pan. Cover loosely with a kitchen towel and let rise in volume. About 45 min. before baking. Preheat oven to 375 degrees. Bake for 45-55 min., or until oaf is golden brown (an instant-read thermometer inserted into center should reach 210 degrees). Remove from oven and cool.

36. Garlic N Herb Monkey Bread Recipe

Serving: 5 | Prep: | Cook: 180mins | Ready in:

Ingredients

- 1 1/3 cups milk
- 2 Tbsp veg oil
- 2 3/4 cups white flour
- 3/4 cup whole wheat flour
- 1 tsp salt
- 1 clove crushed garlic
- 1 tsp sugar
- 3 tsp surebake yeast,
- 1Tbsp butter
- 2 cloves crushed garlic
- 1/4 tsp dry sage
- 1/4 tsp dry rosemary
- 1/2tsp dry basil

Direction

- Place the first 8 ingredients into breadmaker pan in order listed and press setting 8 to make dough.
- Melt butter with garlic and herbs in a saucepan and sauté, set aside.
- When dough is done remove and cut into ten large or twenty small rolls, roll each in butter mix and pile into a baking dish (I use a casserole dish) and place it in a warm spot to rise to double its size.
- Bake at 180c for around 25 to 30 mins till browned.

37. Good For You Garlic Bread Recipe

Serving: 8 | Prep: | Cook: 10mins | Ready in:

Ingredients

- Good quality baguette or sourdough loaf
- olive oil
- Raw garlic, minced or pressed
- Italian herbs (basil, oregano, thyme, and/or rosemary)
- parmesan cheese, freshly grated (optional)

- (Adjust amounts to number of people and individual taste)

Direction

- Pre-heat oven at 350 degrees.
- Slice bread approximately 3/4 inch thick and lay slices on a cookie sheet.
- Drizzle olive oil over each slice.
- Spread raw garlic to taste on each slice.
- Sprinkle slices with herbs and cheese.
- Bake 5-10 minutes, until you can smell the garlic and bread is turning golden.
- If using Parmesan, you might want to broil the bread for a minute or two to brown the cheese.

38. Gorgonzola Garlic Bread Recipe

Serving: 4 | Prep: | Cook: | Ready in:

Ingredients

- 1 loaf of Italian/French bread
- 1 stick unsalted butter
- ½ cup gorgonzola cheese, crumbled
- 1 to 2 cloves fresh garlic, minced
- fresh basil, oregano or parsley (or combo), chopped
- parmigiano-reggiano, freshly grated

Direction

- Cream the butter with the Gorgonzola cheese. Add garlic and whatever chopped herbs you are using.
- Leave loaf whole, but cut slices so that the loaf stays together. Spread cheese mixture in between each slice and reshape loaf. Sprinkle top of loaf with Parmesan cheese and wrap in foil.
- Place in 400°F oven for 10 or 15 minutes and serve hot.

39. Gourmet Garlic Bread Recipe

Serving: 8 | Prep: | Cook: 50mins | Ready in:

Ingredients

- 1 head oven-roasted garlic (see instructions below)
- 1 fresh baguette, sliced about 1 1/2 inches thick (sourdough is the best choice if available)
- ¼-1/2 cup quality olive oil
- 1/2 cup butter, softened
- ½ cup grated parmesan or romano cheese (or a combination of both

Direction

- For the Roasted Garlic:
- Preheat the oven to 400°F.
- Peel off loose outer skin of a garlic head, but leave the skins of the individual cloves intact. Cut off 1/4 to a 1/2 inch of the top of cloves with a sharp knife, exposing the individual cloves of garlic.
- Drizzle garlic liberally with quality olive oil, and wrap in foil. If you use heavy-duty foil, you don't need to put it on a baking sheet. For multiple heads, try baking them in a muffin tin. Bake 30-35 minutes, or until cloves are very soft. It will have a golden color.
- For the Bread:
- Scoop roasted garlic cloves out of skins and mash with half of the softened butter. If it doesn't look like it will be enough, add a little more butter.
- Melt remaining butter and add olive oil (you can experiment with the ratio of oil to butter- everyone's taste is different). Place bread on an ungreased cookie sheet. Brush one side of baguette slices with oil-and-butter combination.
- Next, spread the roasted garlic butter onto the prepared baguette slices. Top with a sprinkle of the grated cheese, and place in 400 degree oven with the rack close to the heat element. Watch bread carefully, and remove when it starts to brown lightly around the edges and cheese is starting to bubble slightly. Very

addictive-but, hey, it's got olive oil and garlic in it, so it must be good for you!

40. Green Olive And Garlic Bread Recipe

Serving: 1012 | Prep: | Cook: 5mins | Ready in:

Ingredients

- 1 loaf French bread (can make your own or store bought)
- 1 garlic clove pressed
- 1 stick of real butter (softened)
- about 12 green olives w/pimento
- 1/8 cup parmesean cheese

Direction

- Slice French loaf in half-length wise.
- Put olives in food processor or chopper and mince well.
- Put butter, pressed garlic, chopped olives, and cheese in a bowl and mix well.
- Spread mixture on both halves of bread.
- Put bread on a baking sheet and put under the broiler on high.
- Let broil until bread is toasted to your liking.
- If you make your own French bread, make sure it is completely cool before spreading the mixture on the bread or it will become gummy/doughy. (Trial & error)

41. Grilled Garlic Bread Recipe

Serving: 12 | Prep: | Cook: 20mins | Ready in:

Ingredients

- 1 cup mayonnaise
- 6 cloves garlis, peeled and minced
- 3/4 cup grated parmesan cheese
- 1/2 cup shredded Cheddar
- 1 tbs half and half 1/4 tsp paprika
- 1 pound loaf French bread, halved lengthwise

Direction

- 1- Preheat grill for med. Heat.
- 2- In a med. bowl, mix the mayonnaise, garlic, and Parmesan cheese. In a saucepan over medium- low heat, mix the Cheddar cheese, half and half, and paprika. Stir constantly until melted and smooth. Pour into the bowl with Mayonnaise mixture, stirring until well blended.
- 3- Place the French bread on the grill cut side down, and let it toast for a few minutes. Remove from the grill, and spread the cheese mixture on each side. Place the halves back to the grill for about 15 mins. turning occasionally, until the loaf is heated through and the cheese mixture is hot.

42. Grilled Garlic Cheese Bread Recipe

Serving: 12 | Prep: | Cook: 20mins | Ready in:

Ingredients

- 1 cup finely shredded cheddar cheese
- 1 stick butter, softened
- 1t chili powder
- 4t garlic powder
- fresh parsley(optional)
- 1lb loaf French or Italian bread, sliced on the diagonal into about 12 slices

Direction

- Combine butter, chili powder and garlic powder and cheese in small bowl.
- Spread butter mixture onto one side of each slice of bread.
- Sprinkle with parsley, if desired

- Form slices into a "loaf" on top of heavy duty aluminum foil (large enough to tightly wrap and seal around entire "loaf" of finished slices)
- Press slices tighter together and wrap in foil.
- Grill using indirect heat for about 20 minutes, turning once during cooking, until slices are crispy.

43. Herb Garlic Bread Recipe

Serving: 8 | Prep: | Cook: 10mins | Ready in:

Ingredients

- 10 medium cloves garlic with skins left on
- 6 tablespoons unsalted butter softened
- 2 tablespoons grated parmesan cheese
- 1/2 teaspoon salt
- 1 tablespoon minced fresh basil
- 1 tablespoon chives
- 1/2 tablespoon minced fresh thyme
- 1/2 tablespoon minced fresh oregano
- 1 pound loaf Italian bread halved lengthwise
- 1/2 teaspoon freshly ground black pepper

Direction

- Adjust oven rack to middle position and heat oven to 500.
- Toast garlic cloves in small skillet over medium heat shaking pan occasionally for 8 minutes.
- When cool enough to handle skin and mince cloves.
- Using fork mash garlic, butter, herbs, cheese and salt in small bowl until thoroughly combined.
- Spread cut sides of loaf evenly with butter mixture then season with pepper.
- Transfer loaf halves buttered side up onto rimmed baking sheet.
- Bake reversing position of baking sheet in oven from front to back halfway through.
- Bake until golden brown and toasted about 10 minutes.
- Cut each half into 2" slices and serve immediately.

44. Home Baked Garlic Naan Bread Recipe

Serving: 2 | Prep: | Cook: 5mins | Ready in:

Ingredients

- 2 cups All purpose flour
- 1 pinch baking powder
- 1 tbs dry yeast
- 2 tbs plain yogurt
- 1 tbs sugar
- 1/2 cup warm water
- 1 tbs oil (veg or olive)
- salt to taste
- 3 cloves chopped garlic
- butter to baste

Direction

- *note that you can add more flour to make it the right consistency. That won't ruin the naan as long as you give it the required 3-4 hours to rise.
- In a mixing bowl add flour, baking powder, salt and sugar.
- Mix well.
- Add your oil and yogurt and mix well.
- Dissolve the yeast in warm water and let it sit for 2 mins.
- Mix the yeast water into your flour and knead well. (Make it a bread dough like consistency and just a little bit sticky. but not too dry, add more water if needed).
- Let it sit for 3-4 hours (I leave it for about 4 hours).
- Knead your dough again for a min or two.
- Divide your dough into 6 parts.
- Turn on your oven to broil and let it heat for 20 mins, with your stone in the oven.
- Make the parts into ball shapes and coat it with flour (makes it easier to roll).

- Sprinkle some chopped garlic on to the ball (you can use, cumin, cilantro, poppy seeds, mustard seeds, almonds, pistachios etc.).
- Using a rolling pin, roll your balls into a pita shape (don't roll it too thin).
- Be careful and put each uncooked naan on the stone and let it cook for 3 mins.
- Check to see if it has puffed up or has a puffy surface.
- Remove from oven and baste it with your melted butter.
- Preserve in foil to keep it warm.
- Repeat the process until you have baked all of your naans.
- Serve with chutney, dry curries or veggies. Eat plain if you like.

45. Jiffy Cheesey Garlic Bread Recipe

Serving: 6 | Prep: | Cook: 8mins |Ready in:

Ingredients

- 1 box Jiffy corn muffin mix
- 1 c self rising flour
- garlic powder
- 1 egg
- 1/4 - 1/2 c milk
- 1 c shredded colby jack cheese

Direction

- Preheat oven to 400.
- Grease round cake pan.
- Pour Jiffy mix into large bowl.
- Add about same about SR Flour (about 1 c).
- Sprinkle with garlic powder.
- Add 1 egg and cheese.
- Add milk, a little at a time, until correct consistency (just a little thicker than cornbread batter).
- Bake according to package directions, until golden brown.

46. Killer Garlic Bread Recipe

Serving: 8 | Prep: | Cook: 15mins |Ready in:

Ingredients

- 1 10" round loaf of Sour Dough bread
- 1 cup mayonnaise
- 1 cup freshly grated parmesan cheese (can use already prepared)
- 1 Tablespoon basil, dried
- 1 teaspoon oregano, dried
- 1 Tablespoon minced onion, dried
- 1 Tablespoon minced fresh parsley
- 3 teaspoons cajun seasoning
- 2-3 Tablespoons minced garlic

Direction

- Slice the loaf in half horizontally.
- Butter cut sides of the bread and toast under the broiler till lightly browned.
- Mix the remaining ingredients and spread over the both halves, using the entire mixture.
- Bake at 400* for 15 min. or until top is brown and puffed.
- Cut into wedges and serve hot.
- You can eat this as a meal along with a salad.
- ENJOY :)

47. Lynne's Retro Garlic Bread Recipe

Serving: 8 | Prep: | Cook: 20mins |Ready in:

Ingredients

- 3 tbs olive oil
- 3 tbs unsalted butter
- 1/4 cup water
- 5 large garlic cloves, minced
- 1 generous tsp dried basil
- 1 generous tsp dried oregano

- 1/4 tsp salt, or to taste
- fresh ground black pepper
- 1 large crusty baguette
- 1 tight-packed cup shredded Asiago or Parmigiano-Reggiano cheese

Direction

- Preheat the oven to 400 degrees. In a small saucepan, combine all the ingredients except the bread and cheese, and set over medium-low heat. When the butter melts, cover the pan and cook for 10 minutes to soften the garlic. Take care not to brown it. Once the garlic is soft, uncover the pan and simmer until you hear the mixture sizzle. Pull pan off the heat.
- Split the bread horizontally. Spread with garlic mixture. Sprinkle each half with cheese. Bake for 15 minutes, or until cheese bubbles. Serve.

48. Mary Megans Garlic Bread Recipe

Serving: 6 | Prep: | Cook: 5mins | Ready in:

Ingredients

- 1 loaf French, italian, or Cuban bread
- 1 tsp garlic powder
- 1 tsp. onion powder
- 1/4 tsp fresh ground black pepper
- salt
- 1/4 cup fine ground parmesan cheese
- 1 or 2 tabls. butter or margarine
- 1 tbls fresh chopped parsley

Direction

- Slice bread loaf length wise open like bun not all the way through. Place on oven sheet. Spread both sides with butter sprinkle both with all spices salt to taste. Cover with cheese lightly both sides. Sprinkle with fresh parsley flakes. Place under broiler until golden brown.

Remove fold together place in oven @ 325 for few min. slice and serve.

49. Marys Garlic Bread Recipe

Serving: 6 | Prep: | Cook: 20mins | Ready in:

Ingredients

- 1 cup butter, softened
- 1 cup grated parmesan cheese
- ½ cup mayonnaise
- 5 cloves fresh garlic minced or pressed
- 3 tablespoons chopped fresh parsley
- ½ teaspoon oregano
- 1 large loaf French bread, cut lengthwise

Direction

- Mix all ingredients in bowl and spread on bread.
- Wrap in foil and bake at 375 degrees for 20 minutes.
- Unwrap and brown slightly under the broiler.
- Michele also sprinkles paprika on the bread before putting under broiler.
- Italian bread can be substituted for French bread.

50. Moms Delicious Garlic Bread Recipe

Serving: 8 | Prep: | Cook: 8mins | Ready in:

Ingredients

- Loaf of Italian bread
- olive oil (no other oil will do)
- garlic salt
- garlic powder
- paprika

Direction

- Place oven on "broil".
- Slice the loaf of bread through into disks 3/4 - 1 inch thick.
- Pour olive oil into a saucer and dip each disk (both sides) into the oil.
- Place onto a cookie sheet.
- Sprinkle each with garlic salt, garlic powder, and paprika.
- Turn over and sprinkle the other side.
- Place on middle rack in your oven. Broil for approx. 4 mins on first side until golden.
- Turn over and broil for approx. 4 mins more until golden. Time will vary according to your oven.
- Watch it carefully, do not allow to burn.

51. Onion And Garlic Bread Recipe

Serving: 4 | Prep: | Cook: 18mins | Ready in:

Ingredients

- 1 tablespoon butter
- 1 medium onion, yellow skinned, chopped
- 3 cloves garlic, crushed
- 1 teaspoon sugar
- 1/2 teaspoon ground thyme, poultry seasoning may be substituted
- A few grinds black pepper
- 1 (12-inch) loaf crusty bread, split lengthwise
- 2 handfuls grated parmigiano

Direction

- Melt butter in a small pan over moderate heat.
- Add onions and garlic and season with sugar, thyme and pepper. Cook 15 minutes, stirring occasionally, until onions are golden in color and translucent.
- Place the split bread on a baking sheet and broil until golden. Spread half the onions and garlic on each half of bread in a thin layer.
- Sprinkle each side of loaf with a handful of cheese and return to broiler for 30 seconds to bubble cheese.
- Serve with a hearty, soup-er supper.

52. PROVOLONE GARLIC BREAD Recipe

Serving: 4 | Prep: | Cook: 6mins | Ready in:

Ingredients

- 3 tb extra-virgin olive oil
- 3 garlic cloves, peeled, -ends removed, minced
- 4 lg Thick slices of crusty bread
- 4 Slices (1 1/2 ounces each) -provolone cheese
- 1/4 c Freshly grated Parmesan -cheese

Direction

- For garlic bread, mix olive oil and garlic in a small bowl and let stand 10 minutes so the flavors blend. Meanwhile, heat broiler. Brush one side of each bread piece with the garlic/olive oil mixture, and broil, oiled side up, until lightly browned. Place a slice of provolone and a generous sprinkling of Parmesan on toasted side of each slice, saving a little for garnish. Set the bread aside.
- Just before serving, heat the broiler. Toast the bread under the broiler until cheese is bubbly.
- ....
- Serve with soup or stew or with the marinated cherry tomato recipe as an appetizer spoon some of the tomatoes on top and serve. Garnish with a thin curl of Parmesan cheese.

53. Parmesan And Asiago Cheese Garlic Bread Recipe

Serving: 8 | Prep: | Cook: 10mins | Ready in:

Ingredients

- 9 - 10 medium cloves garlic (about the size of a plump cashew nut), skins left on

- 1/4 cup grated asiago cheese
- 2 teaspoons Dijon mustard
- 6 tablespoons unsalted butter, softened
- 1/4 cups grated parmesan cheese
- 1/4 teaspoon table salt
- 1 loaf Italian bread (high-quality; about 1 pound, football-shaped), halved lengthwise
- ground black pepper

Direction

- Note:
- Garlic bread is best served piping hot, so time it to arrive at the table last, once all the other dishes are finished and ready to serve.
- 1. Adjust oven rack to middle position and heat oven to 500 degrees. Meanwhile, toast garlic cloves in small skillet over medium heat, shaking pan occasionally, until fragrant and color of cloves deepens slightly, about 8 minutes. When cool enough to handle, skin and mince cloves (you should have about 3 tablespoons). Using dinner fork, mash garlic, Asiago cheese, Dijon, butter, cheese, and salt in small bowl until thoroughly combined.
- 2. Spread cut sides of loaf evenly with garlic butter mixture; season to taste with pepper. Transfer loaf halves, buttered side up, onto baking sheet; bake, reversing position of baking sheet in oven from front to back halfway through baking time, until surface of bread is golden brown and toasted, 8 to 10 minutes. Cut each half into 2-inch slices; serve immediately.
- Note: Garlic Bread Techniques:
- Toast the unpeeled garlic cloves in a small, dry skillet over medium-high heat for 8 minutes, tossing frequently. Using a long serrated knife, slice the bread in half lengthwise.

54. Parmesan Garlic Bread Recipe

Serving: 12 | Prep: | Cook: 50mins | Ready in:

Ingredients

- 1 French loaf
- garlic salt or powder
- butter
- parmesan cheese

Direction

- With a sharp knife cut the French loaf down the middle LENGTHWISE, to about two inches of each end.
- Then, without cutting completely through the loaf, cut it into two inch slices as you would if you were simply cutting slices of the bread. Try not to cut completely through the bottom of the slices as you want the cheese and butter to stay in the loaf.
- Open the loaf up as much as you can without tearing it apart and butter all exposed soft bread, not only the tops, but getting down and buttering the sides, too, but leaving crust unbuttered.
- Once bread is buttered, you can liberally sprinkle it with garlic and parmesan cheese, trying again to get the sides as well as the top.
- Make a long bowl for your loaf out of tin foil and set your loaf in it.
- Melt a cup of butter and pour it over the parmesan cheese. Don't worry if all of the bread is not covered with the melted butter it isn't supposed to be.
- Completely cover the loaf with tin foil and bake in a 350F oven for approximately 40 or 50 minutes.
- Remove from oven, remove the top tin foil covering, leaving the loaf in the tin foil bowl you made before baking and serve, allowing people to pull pieces of the bread from the loaf themselves.

55. Parmesan And Asiago Cheese Garlic Bread Recipe

Serving: 8 | Prep: | Cook: 10mins | Ready in:

Ingredients

- 10 medium cloves garlic with skins left on
- 6 tablespoons unsalted butter softened
- 1/4 cup grated parmesan cheese
- 1/4 cup grated asiago cheese
- 2 teaspoons spicy mustard
- 1/4 teaspoon salt
- 1 pound loaf Italian bread halved lengthwise
- 1/2 teaspoon freshly ground black pepper

Direction

- Adjust oven rack to middle position and heat oven to 500.
- Toast garlic cloves in small skillet over medium heat shaking pan occasionally for 8 minutes.
- When cool enough to handle skin and mince cloves.
- Using fork mash garlic, butter, cheeses, mustard and salt in bowl until thoroughly combined.
- Spread cut sides of loaf evenly with butter mixture then season with pepper.
- Transfer loaf halves buttered side up onto rimmed baking sheet.
- Bake reversing position of baking sheet in oven from front to back halfway through.
- Bake until golden brown and toasted about 10 minutes.
- Cut each half into 2" slices and serve immediately.

56. Quick Easy Garlic Bread Sticks Recipe

Serving: 12 | Prep: | Cook: 20mins | Ready in:

Ingredients

- 3 cups flour
- 1 teaspoon salt
- 1 teaspoon garlic powder
- 1 tablespoon dry parsley (optional, for decoration)
- 1 tablespoon baking powder
- 1 cup milk
- 1/2 cup margarine (1 stick)
- 1 more teaspoon garlic powder
- 1/2 teaspoon salt (optional)

Direction

- Begin with your favorite big bowl. Measure your flour, salt, garlic powder, parsley and baking powder into it. Stir the dry ingredients together so that the salt, garlic powder, parsley and baking powder are evenly distributed throughout the flour. Now pour in your milk. Stir with a big spoon until you get a ball of dough that leaves the sides of the bowl. You may have to dust the ball of dough with a little flour if it seems sticky to you. Gently knead the ball of dough right there in the bowl about 5 or 6 times. Now place your dough on the counter. You may place a sheet of waxed paper under it you like. Using a rolling pin or sturdy bottle roll the dough out into a rectangle shape. If the edges get all scraggly then use your hands to press them back up into main rectangle. Sometimes I simply take the dough and press it into the pan to form its shape and then remove it. It doesn't have to be perfect.
- Meanwhile place the margarine in a 9 by 13-inch pan. Place the pan in the oven at 425°. Allow the pan to preheat and the margarine to melt. When the margarine is melted, carefully remove the pan from the oven. It will be very hot, so don't burn yourself. Sprinkle the second teaspoon of garlic powder and the 1/2-teaspon of salt into the pan. You do not have to use the extra salt. We like our bread sticks salty so I always use it, but it isn't vital. Now, very carefully lay your rectangle of dough into the pan, over top of the margarine. Next cut the rectangle into narrow strips. I use a pizza cutter for this because it seems to work the best. A sharp knife will work too though, so use what you

have available. My method of cutting is to cut the dough in half and then cut each half in half and then each quarter in half, going on and on until I have a lot of narrow strips of dough. The margarine will creep up between the strips. This is normal. It is what gives these bread sticks their texture. After cutting your strips, place the pan in the oven, still at 425°, and bake them for 20 minutes. They will be brown and crispy when they are done.

57. Quick Casserole Garlic Bread Recipe

Serving: 12 | Prep: | Cook: 60mins | Ready in:

Ingredients

- 5 tbsp salted butter
- 4 cloves garlic, minced
- 2 cups flour
- 1 1/2 cups whole wheat flour
- 4 tsp baking powder
- 1 egg
- 1 1/2 cups nonfat milk

Direction

- Preheat oven to 350F. Lightly grease a 2-qt casserole dish and set aside.
- Melt 1 tbsp. butter in a small pan.
- Add garlic and cook gently 3 minutes, do not let it brown. Set aside.
- Blend all dry ingredients in a large bowl.
- Cut in 3 tbsp. butter to resemble crumbs.
- Beat together egg, milk and the garlic butter, add to the dry mix and blend well.
- Knead on a floured board 10-20 minutes, until not sticky.
- Shape bread into a round and place in the casserole.
- Slash the top of the round 1-2 times.
- Melt the final tablespoon of butter and brush the loaf generously.
- Bake 1 hour, then cool in the pan 10 minutes before turning out onto a rack.

58. Quick Garlic Cheese Bread Recipe

Serving: 0 | Prep: | Cook: 10mins | Ready in:

Ingredients

- 3 tablespoons mayonnaise
- 1 tablespoon grated parmesan cheese
- 1 garlic clove, minced
- 1 dash paprika
- 2 tablespoons finely shredded cheddar cheese
- 2 French bread rolls, halved lengthwise

Direction

- In a small bowl, combine the mayonnaise, Parmesan cheese, garlic and paprika; stir in cheddar cheese.
- Place rolls cut side up on a baking sheet; broil 6 in. from the heat for 1 minute or until lightly browned.
- Spread with cheese mixture. Broil 1 minute longer or until bubbly and lightly browned.
- Enjoy with Pasta or any of your favourite dishes!

59. Quick Italian Garlic Bread Slices Recipe

Serving: 6 | Prep: | Cook: 3mins | Ready in:

Ingredients

- 6 slices of favorite bread
- 1/2 stick butter, melted
- 1 tablespoon italian seasoning
- 1 tablespoon garlic powder
- dash of grated parmesan cheese

Direction

- Melt butter in microwave.
- Mix in the Italian seasoning, garlic powder and Parmesan cheese.
- Brush over bread and place under the broiler until lightly browned.
- Remove bread and brush other side.
- Place under the broiler until lightly browned
- Remove and cut each piece of bread into 3 or 4 strips.
- It's that easy! Adjust amounts of spices and cheese to taste.

60. Quick, Easy, Delicious Garlic Bread Recipe

Serving: 0 | Prep: | Cook: 30mins | Ready in:

Ingredients

- 1 loaf French or Italian bread
- Variation 1:
- 6oz butter, melted
- garlic powder or Garlic spread or garlic salt
- 1/2 Tbsp parsley, chopped (ONLY if using either garlic powder or garlic salt. Garlic spread has herbs in it.)
- shredded mozzarella (optional)
- Variation2:
- 6oz butter, melted
- 3 Large garlic cloves, crushed and chopped
- 1/2 Tbsp parsley, chopped.
- shredded mozzarella (optional)

Direction

- Slice bread loaf in half, lengthwise, with a serrated bread knife.
- Pre-heat oven to 350 degrees
- Variation 1:
- With pastry brush, brush half of melted butter on inside of one half of the loaf. Brush the rest of the butter on the other half.
- Sprinkle garlic powder/garlic salt/garlic spread (PICK ONE!) all over the bread where it is buttered. Be careful not to use too much!
- Sprinkle parsley evenly over garlic and butter.
- If desired, sprinkle shredded mozzarella evenly over garlic, butter, and parsley.
- Wrap bread halves in foil and place on a half sheet tray.
- Bake in oven for 15-20 minutes or until edges of bread are slightly toasted.
- Variation 2:
- Mix minced garlic in a small bowl with the butter.
- With a pastry brush, brush half of the melted butter/garlic mixture on the inside of one half of the loaf. Brush the rest of the butter on the other half.
- Sprinkle parsley evenly over garlic and butter.
- If desired, sprinkle shredded mozzarella evenly over garlic, butter, and parsley.
- Wrap bread halves in foil and place on a half sheet tray.
- Bake in oven for 15-20 minutes or until edges of bread are slightly toasted.
- **NOTE: Makes a perfect side dish for literally ANY Italian dish.

61. Reenies Garlic Bread Recipe

Serving: 6 | Prep: | Cook: 20mins | Ready in:

Ingredients

- 2 tsp. garlic, finely chopped
- 1/4 tsp. kosher salt
- 1/2 stick butter, unsalted preferably and softened
- 1 tbls. extra virgin olive oil
- 2 tbls. parsley or basil, finely chopped
- 1 loaf Italian bread

Direction

- Preheat oven to 350.

- With knife, mash garlic and salt together to make paste.
- In small mixing bowl, mix together butter, olive oil, and garlic paste.
- Mix in parley or basil.
- Cut bread diagonally into 1 in. thick slices without cutting completely through bottom of bread.
- Spread garlic butter between slices.
- Wrap in foil.
- Bake for 15 minutes.
- Open foil and bake 5 more minutes.

62. Roasted Garlic Bread Recipe

Serving: 6 | Prep: | Cook: 30mins | Ready in:

Ingredients

- 1 loaf rustic French or Italian bread
- 1/2 cup roasted garlic
- 1 tablespoon roasted garlic cooking oil
- coarse salt and ground pepper

Direction

- Preheat oven to 400. In a small bowl, mash roasted garlic and cooking oil to a coarse paste with a fork.
- Split the bread horizontally and spread garlic paste on both sides. Season generously with salt and pepper. Place bread on a rimmed baking sheet and bake until garlic is golden and edges of bread are crisp, ~25 minutes. Cut into wedges for serving.

63. Roasted Garlic Potato Bread Recipe

Serving: 12 | Prep: | Cook: 35mins | Ready in:

Ingredients

- 4 cups King Arthur all-purpose flour
- 1/4 cup potato flour (not potato starch)
- 2 teaspoons instant yeast
- 2 teaspoons pizza seasoning
- 1 1/4 teaspoons salt
- 1 1/2 cups water
- 2 tablespoons olive oil
- 1 head (8 to 10 cloves) garlic, baked
- 1 1/2 to 2 cups (16 to 18 ounces raw weight) diced (1/2-inch chunks) roasted potatoes, peeled or not

Direction

- Combine the flour, potato flour, yeast, Pizza Seasoning, salt, water and olive oil, and mix and knead them together-by hand, mixer or bread machine-till you've made a soft, smooth dough. Remove the baked garlic from its skin by gently squeezing. Knead in the garlic and then the potatoes. Allow the dough to rise, covered, for 1 1/2 to 2 hours, until it's doubled.
- Turn the dough out onto a lightly greased surface and knead it gently to deflate it, then shape it into a ball. Some potatoes may pop out-that's fine. Place the loaf into a lightly greased 9- to 10-inch round baker or cake pan (this will help the bread rise in an even shape), or onto a baking sheet. Cover with lightly greased plastic wrap or a proof cover, and let the loaf rise for 1 to 1 1/2 hours.
- Preheat your oven to 375°F. Just before placing the bread in the oven, gently score the top of the bread about 1/2-inch deep in a grid pattern, and spritz it with water. Bake the bread for 32 to 38 minutes, until it's deeply browned. Remove it from the oven, turn it out of the pan, and cool it on a rack before slicing. Yield: 1 large loaf

64. Roman Garlic Bread Recipe

Serving: 10 | Prep: | Cook: 5mins | Ready in:

Ingredients

- 1/2 cup butter
- 1/2 teaspoon garlic salt
- 3 teaspoons chopped parsley
- 1/2 teaspoon oregano
- 2 tablespoon fresh grated parmesan cheese
- 1 loaf French bread (cut in slices)

Direction

- Combine all ingredients except bread.
- Let stand for 20 to 30 minutes.
- Brush bread slices with butter mixture.
- Broil until brown and bubbling.
- Serve immediately.

65. Simple Garlic Bread Recipe

Serving: 0 | Prep: | Cook: 5mins | Ready in:

Ingredients

- garlic powder
- hot dog buns
- margarine

Direction

- Butter your hot dog buns.
- Sprinkle a light dusting of the garlic powder on it.
- Pop it in the microwave for about 32sec.
- Take it out and enjoy!

66. Soft Garlic Breadsticks Recipe

Serving: 0 | Prep: | Cook: 1hours | Ready in:

Ingredients

- 1 1/8 cups water (70-80 degrees F)
- 2 tablespoons olive or canola oil
- 3 tablespoons grated parmesan cheese
- 2 tablespoons sugar
- 4 teaspoons garlic powder
- 1 1/2 teaspoons salt
- 3/4 teaspoon minced fresh basil
- 3 cups bread flour
- 2 teaspoons active dry yeast
- 1 tablespoon butter or stick margarine, melted

Direction

- 1. In the bread machine pan place the first 9 ingredients in order as recommended by the manufacturer.
- 2. Select dough setting (check after about 5 minutes of mixing, add 1-2 tablespoons of water or flour if needed)
- 3. When dough is finished turn on to a lightly floured surface.
- 4. Divide into 20 portions.
- 5. Shape each into a ball, roll into a 9 in rope, and then place on greased baking sheet.
- 6. Cover and let rise in a warm place for 40 minutes or until doubled.
- 7. Bake at 350 degrees F for 18-232 minutes or until golden brown.
- 8. Remove to wire racks.
- 9. Brush warm breadsticks with butter.
- If you don't want to cook them all now then you can freeze them and pull them out when you need them, bake and brush with melted butter.

67. Sourdough Garlic Bread Recipe

Serving: 12 | Prep: | Cook: 10mins | Ready in:

Ingredients

- butter
- garlic powder
- dried basil
- 12 Slices of sourdough bread
- 3-4 cloves of garlic Minced

Direction

- Preheat oven to 400 and set out a cookie sheet.
- Cut and peel garlic and then mince.
- In a small or medium sauce pan melt the butter then mix in the garlic powder and basil.
- Carefully lay the bread slice into the mixture then quickly flip it with your fingers by grabbing the edges. Then move to cookie sheet and sprinkle with minced garlic.
- Repeat until they are all ready to bake.
- Put in the oven for 10 minutes, flip after 5 minutes so the garlic will be toasted.

68. Stuffed Garlic Spinach Bread Recipe

Serving: 6 | Prep: | Cook: 20mins | Ready in:

Ingredients

- 2 tablespoons extra-virgin olive oil, divided
- 1 large onion, finely chopped
- 3 cloves garlic, minced
- 1 can (14.5 ounces) no-salt-added chopped, spinach, drained and squeezed dry
- 1/2 cup diced, canned red bell peppers (pimentos)
- 12 large black olives, chopped (optional)
- Pinch crushed red pepper
- 1/4 cup freshly grated parmesan cheese, divided
- kosher salt and ground black pepper, to taste
- 1 pound frozen pizza dough, thawed

Direction

- Preheat oven to 425°F.
- Heat 1 tablespoon olive oil in a large skillet over medium-high heat. Add onion and sauté until tender, about 3 minutes. Add garlic and stir 30 seconds. Remove from heat and stir in spinach, peppers, olives, crushed pepper, 3 tablespoons Parmesan cheese, salt and pepper.
- Roll out pizza dough into a 12-inch round using just enough flour on the work surface and dough to keep it from sticking. Brush off excess flour and transfer dough to a baking sheet. Sprinkle remaining Parmesan cheese over the center and mound the spinach mixture on one side of the dough leaving a 1/2-inch border of exposed dough at the edge. Brush the exposed edge with water, and fold the other side of the dough over top, stretching it so that it completely encases the filling. Firmly pinch the edges together sealing the filling inside. Cut 4 slits in the top and brush with remaining olive oil. Bake until crisp and brown, about 20 minutes; cool 10 minutes before serving. Cut in 6 wedges.
- Nutritional Information Per Serving(without olives): Calories 350; Total fat 10g; Saturated fat 1.5g; Cholesterol 5mg; Sodium 780mg; Total carbohydrate 50g; Fiber 3g; Protein 12g; Vitamin A 40%DV*; Vitamin C 35%DV; Calcium 15%DV; Iron 20%DV
- * Daily Value
- Serving size: 1 slice (with 2.5 ounces bread plus filling)

69. Summy Wummys Famous Garlic Bread Recipe

Serving: 5 | Prep: | Cook: 10mins | Ready in:

Ingredients

- 1 stick of butter
- 2-3 cloves of garlic
- 1 loaf of French bread, cut in half the long way
- 1/2 cp parm cheese (the real stuff)'

Direction

- Oven to 350 degrees.
- Line a baking tray with foil.
- Melt the butter in a small bowl in the microwave just until soft.
- Peel and press the garlic.

- Stir the garlic into the softened butter.
- With a brush or spoon spread the garlic butter over each half of the loaf of bread.
- Sprinkle the parmesan evenly over the top.
- Bake in the oven until the garlic bread is golden-brown on top and crispy on the outside (10 to 15mins).

70. Tear N Share Garlic Pizza Bread By Hand Or Machine Recipe

Serving: 4 | Prep: | Cook: 15mins | Ready in:

Ingredients

- This is suitable for making by hand or bread machine. Simply add ingredients to you machine in the order instructed in the manual. Set the machine to Dough or Pizza setting but you must rest the dough for 45 minutes further or more if you have time. Or if making by hand, see below:
- 1/2 tsp dried yeast powder
- 11oz (300gms) Strong white flour (ideally strong bread flour)
- 1/2 tsp white granulated sugar
- 1/2 oz (15g) butter
- 1 tbsp milk Powder (this is trick (i) to make it rise & airy)
- 1 tsp salt
- 7fl oz (210ml) luke warm water
- Choose between:
- fresh basil, oregano, parsley, dill: or
- Italian mixed dried herbs
- 2oz Low fat spread or butter for blending with the herb topping
- 1 tbsp garlic granules or 3 crushed & diced garlic cloves

Direction

- There are 2 tricks (I call them that because they make a huge difference in the outcome).
- Add the dried yeast to a little of the water, and mix the paste then leave for 15 minutes to work together. When the liquid has a frothy surface then it's ready to use.
- While waiting for the yeast to work, mix the flour, sugar, salt and Milk Powder (I) together and make sure it is well mixed
- Melt the butter in the microwave and add it to the remaining water (which should still be lukewarm.
- Add the liquids to the dry mix and use a hard spatula or spoon to mix ingredients together, then when the mix starts to look like a dough, use your hands to work it together.
- Heavily flour your work surface and knead the dough for a good 10 to 15 minutes, add more flour if the mix is too wet, as the Milk Powder will compensate.
- Shape the dough in the way you want it, then place onto an edgeless baking sheet or a baking board that you can easily slide the bread from, onto a pizza stone or baking tray. Heavily coat the base of the sheet or tray or stone with semolina, as this acts as like wee ball bearings and helps the shift from the dough's resting place to the baking sheet.
- (ii) LEAVE THE DOUGH TO RISE FOR AT LEAST 1 HOUR or more if you have time. Make the dough in the morning if you want, for baking at night
- Preheat your oven to (220c/425f gas mark 7) with the sheet or stone in the oven for at least 30 minutes, or better up to 45 minutes.
- Melt the butter add the chopped fresh or dried herbs, and garlic, mix well and then very quickly coat the top of the bread with using a pastry brush and then transfer the bread to your pre-heated baking sheet/stone.
- Slip into the oven on the middle shelf.
- If it has not puffed up, allow an extra 3 to 5 minutes.

71. The Best Ever Two Minute Fake Garlic Bread Recipe

Serving: 1 | Prep: | Cook: 2mins | Ready in:

Ingredients

- clove of garlic
- herbs
- bread
- butter
- Grated motzarella cheese

Direction

- Toast the bread.
- Cut the garlic clove in half, rub the cut side on the dry toast.
- Butter the bread, and sprinkle with herbs (I used thyme as it's my favourite but mix herbs or oregano works well too.)
- Sprinkle sparingly with the grated cheese put under the grill till cheese is melted.

72. Ukrainian Garlic Bread Puffs Recipe

Serving: 12 | Prep: | Cook: 5mins | Ready in:

Ingredients

- 1 cup warm water
- 1 pkg. dry yeast
- 2 Tbs. sugar
- 3 cup flour
- 1 tsp salt
- 2 Tbs oil
- 3 cloves garlic, peeled and mashed with salt, or prepared garlic salt (I prefer kosher salt and real garlic crushed)

Direction

- Dissolve yeast in water, add sugar, and allow to foam.
- Combine flour, salt, salt, oil, and yeast mixture and knead into dough.
- Place in a lightly greased bowl, cover with plastic wrap or towel, allow to double in size.
- Punch down, pinch off small pieces of dough, roll between lightly oiled palm into 1 inch balls, and place on floured towel.
- Heat at least 2 inches of oil in a skillet until hot but not smoking. Drop in dough balls, fry on all sides, remove and drain on paper towels. Roll in or sprinkle with garlic salt.
- Serve warm.
- Enjoy.

73. Garlic Bread By The Slice Recipe

Serving: 2 | Prep: | Cook: 57mins | Ready in:

Ingredients

- sliced french or Italian bread about an inch thick (2 slices or more)
- 1/4 cup of butter (i use unsalted, the parmesan is salty)
- 3 cloves of minced garlic (i use a garlic press)
- 3 to 4 tablespoons of parmesan cheese
- dash of red pepper flakes (optional, i like the hit of heat)

Direction

- Preheat broiler to 350 or low. (My broiler is on top so I adjust the oven rack to the 2nd from the top).
- In a Pyrex measuring cup mince the garlic and add the butter and the dash of red pepper flakes (optional). Microwave until bubbly.
- Brush the butter garlic mixture onto each slice of bread.
- Top with parmesan cheese.
- Broil until desired brownness (is that a word??) LOL.
- I like mine golden with a little more brown on the edges.
- Enjoy.
- Please be careful, this burns really easy. I cannot tell you how many times I have

forgotten I had this in the broiler and had to make it over.
- Live and learn right?

74. Garlic Cheese Bread Recipe

Serving: 4 | Prep: | Cook: 12mins | Ready in:

Ingredients

- One loaf of store bought French bread
- 3 good-sized garlic cloves, minced
- 1 stick of unsalted butter, softened
- 1 Tbsp mayonnaisse
- 1-1/2 Cups 6-cheese italian blend shredded cheese (I use sargento's)

Direction

- Preheat oven to 375 F. Combine butter, garlic and mayonnaise, mix until smooth. Slice bread horizontally, spread both sides evenly with butter mixture. Sprinkle cheese over the two halves and place onto a cookie sheet lined with aluminum foil. Place in oven and bake until cheese is slightly brown and bubbly. Slice into 2 inch slices and serve.

75. Roasted Garlic And Rosemary Bread Recipe

Serving: 1 | Prep: | Cook: 35mins | Ready in:

Ingredients

- 1 1/2 c. hot water
- 2 T yeast
- 2 c. white flour
- 2 c. wheat flour
- 1 tsp. salt
- 4 T olive oil
- optional 3 cloves minced garlic
- optional 2T fresh minced rosemary
- optional additional 2T olive oil

Direction

- Dissolve yeast in hot water.
- Mix the flour, salt and olive in large bowl.
- Add yeast/water mixture and stir together.
- Dump out on floured surface and knead until smooth and elastic.
- Let rise until doubled in size (approximately 1 hour).
- Punch down dough, knead slightly and form into loaf (you can use a loaf pan or roll it into a long loaf as in French).
- Bake at 375 for 35 minutes.
- For roasted garlic and rosemary variation, put minced garlic and rosemary in olive and bake at 200 for about 30minutes while bread rises. Add this during the second kneading.

Index

A
Artichoke 3,9

B
Banana 3,6

Basil 3,6

Bread 1,3,4,5,6,7,8,9,10,11,12,13,14,15,16,17,18,19,20,21,22,23,24,25,26,27,28,29,30,31,32,33,34,35

Butter 11,23,31,34

C
Caramel 3,8

Cheddar 3,14,21

Cheese 3,7,8,13,14,15,16,21,23,25,26,28,35

Cream 20

D
Dijon mustard 9,26

Dill 13

F
Flour 23

Focaccia 3,6

French bread 7,11,12,13,14,15,20,21,24,28,31,32,35

G
Garlic 1,3,4,5,6,7,8,9,10,11,12,13,14,15,16,17,18,19,20,21,22,23,24,25,26,27,28,29,30,31,32,33,34,35

Gorgonzola 3,20

H
Herbs 3,13

J
Jus 11,25,30

M
Mayonnaise 21

Milk 33

Mince 31

Mozzarella 3,5

N
Nut 12,32

O
Oil 13,14,18

Olive 3,6,13,14,21

Onion 3,8,10,25

P
Parmesan 3,9,10,16,17,20,21,25,26,28,29,32

Pasta 28

Peel 6,20,32

Pizza 3,30,33

Port 11

Potato 3,18,30

R
Rosemary 3,4,18,35

S
Seasoning 30

Spinach 3,32

Strong white flour 33

T
Tea 3,33

Tomato 3,15

W

Walnut 3,18

Worcestershire sauce 9

L

lasagna 12

Conclusion

Thank you again for downloading this book!

I hope you enjoyed reading about my book!

If you enjoyed this book, please take the time to share your thoughts and post a review on Amazon. It'd be greatly appreciated!

Write me an honest review about the book – I truly value your opinion and thoughts and I will incorporate them into my next book, which is already underway.

Thank you!

If you have any questions, **feel free to contact at:** *author@bisquerecipes.com*

Alice Francis

bisquerecipes.com

Printed in Great Britain
by Amazon